Vancouver Island Birds

by mike yip

volume II

Yellow Warbler at Buttertubs Marsh

Contents

Canadian Cataloguing in Publication Data

Yip, Mike 1943 -

Vancouver Island Birds (Volume II)
A photographic celebration of the birds of
Vancouver Island

Includes bibliographic references and index
ISBN 0-9738161-1-2

1. Vancouver Island Birds (Volume I)
0-9738161-0-4

Mike Yip
1884 Stewart Road
Nanoose Bay, B.C. V9P 9E7

http://vancouverislandbirds.com

Printed in Canada

Double-crested Cormorant at French Creek

Prologue

Almost 200 years ago the romantic poet, John Keats, penned the memorable line:

"A thing of beauty is a joy for ever."

I first encountered Keats' poem during my high school days in Lake Cowichan over 40 years ago. For some unknown reason his words have been indelibly etched in my mind ever since. Perhaps it is because I see the beauty and experience the joy of nature and the birds every day. It doesn't matter if it's my backyard Chestnut-backed Chickadee or the rarely seen Gray-crowned Rosy Finch at Clover Point. Each is beautiful in its own right.

Beauty and joy is one thing, but obsession is another. How can I account for my preoccupation with birds for the past four years? The answer is simple. Birds are fascinating. They can fly. They can defy gravity. Some can even fly and swim. They are master navigators. Without the benefit of compasses or GPS, they can travel thousands of kilometers to precise locations. Shorebirds born in the Arctic don't even need their parents for their long distance migrations. Birds have many other amazing skills and abilities to survive in difficult situations.

On the other hand, I would love to fly, but I can't; I have difficulty navigating out of the parking lot at the shopping mall; and my survival skills are limited to the use of a credit card. Need I say more? I feel inadequate and totally humbled in the presence of birds. I am like a groupie to a rock star or a sycophant to a genius. I want to learn more about them, but the more I learn, the less I know. Each answer only leads to more questions. However, I am patient. I am willing to learn, one mistake at a time.

Long-billed Dowitcher at Holden Creek

Photography

I am grateful to have the ability and means to photograph birds, but it is not an end in itself. Firstly, it gives me an excuse to be out in nature, and nature is my classroom. I see how the birds forage, preen, interact, and react to predators and strangers. Secondly, it gives me another chance to study the feathers and specialized structures more thoroughly as I enlarge their images on the computer. I can study the details without having to worry about exposure, ISO, or depth of field. Thirdly, it allows me relive and enjoy the experiences vicariously many times over as I am reminded of each encounter. Finally, it allows me to share my experiences with others and contribute to conservation and educational efforts all over the world. A few examples include my Swainson's Thrush photo for an environmental education program in Peru; Red Crossbill photo for a local nature reserve project in Halton, England; White-winged Scoter photo for a Nature Society project in Turkey; and American Dipper photos for the Yuba Kid's Club in the Sierra Nevadas.

I know my photos, website, book, and presentations have made positive contributions to educating the public about birds and nature. It is the least I can do. The destruction of the natural world continues at an alarming rate. It is incumbent upon us to do as much as we can to ensure that there will be a natural world for our children and generations to follow. I understand the feeling of helplessness when confronted with such a massive problem. It is easy to be numbed into complacency, but doing something is better than nothing. Even cutting down on our consumption of fossil fuels, electrical energy, water, and material goods will help - flush less, consume less, turn out the lights ...

Heermann's Gulls at Clover Point

To Publish or Not to Publish?

Less than two years ago I was agonizing over whether I should gamble on self-publishing "Vancouver Island Birds - Volume I." The financial risk was substantial not to mention the time and effort. However, the goal of my photography and website was to increase public awareness of our birds and the natural world. The goal would be the same for a book. Not everyone uses the internet. Some still don't have computers. My book would be reaching out to a new audience. That was reason enough to proceed. It was worth the gamble. Could I produce a publication that was intersting, artistically appealing, and marketable? I had some good photographs and previous experience as a yearbook sponsor at Ballenas Secondary. I was confident that I could design and produce a quality book. The biggest obstacle was marketing. Could I sell 3,000 books? There was only one way to find out.

I had always been happy with Friesens Corporation for yearbooks and didn't hesitate in choosing them as my printer. After preliminary discussions with Gerhard Aichelberger regarding printing specs and costs and Brad Schmidt for technical information, I decided the project was viable. It was time to buy a new computer and the proper software. By April 1, 2005, I was comfortable with the idea of publishing and committed to designing and producing the book. Six weeks later my completed DVD was in Friesens' plant in Manitoba, and by the last week of June, 3,000 books landed in my driveway.

It was time to put on my marketing hat. The response from my personal contacts was sensational, and I was truly grateful: everybody from the Royal Bank in Parksville bought a copy; residents at Craig

Pileated Woodpecker in my garden (Nanoose)

Bay re-ordered several times; Fairwinds members were extremely supportive; and schools like Ballenas remembered me. That gave me the confidence to approach the newspapers and bookstores. Local papers from Victoria to Campbell River carried book reviews and articles, and I was interviewed by Bruce Williams on the A-Channel Morning Show. Most booksellers on the Island were more than happy to stock the book. Surprisingly, my best outlets were in the north Island. Blue Heron Books in Comox and Save-On Foods in Campbell River regularly re-ordered books, but the biggest seller wasn't even a bookstore. It was Graham's Jewellers in Courtenay. They sold twice as many as any bookstore.

I am grateful for the success of Volume I and the encouragement for Volume II. Finding enough new birds to photograph would have been impossible without a lot of help. I am thankful for those who reported birds like the Northern Wheatear and Bar-tailed Godwit on the V.I. Yahoo birding sites. I am grateful to those who invited me to their backyards like Melanee Mole for the Blue Jay and Ted Ardley for the Clay-coloured and White-throated Sparrows. Last but not least, I am forever indebted to Ron and Hetty Mann for 13 days in pelagic heaven on their OSPREY I fishing boat. Besides 15 new bird species, it was the experience of a lifetime I'll never forget.

"Beauty is in the eyes of the beholder," and I am hoping that Volume II will also be "a thing of beauty and a joy for ever."

May the birds be with you,
Mike Yip
March, 2007

female Common Merganser at French Creek

Holden Creek

It is smelly, slimy, and slippery, and the mosquitoes are horrendous, but it is my favorite spot for shorebirds. The shallow, brackish puddles left after high tide are the perfect habitat for migrating shorebirds. Oh yes, for mosquitoes as well, but you can't have it all. It is a small price to pay for the opportunity to enjoy one of the best shorebird viewing spots on Vancouver Island.

shorebirds

shorebirds at Holden Creek

Bar-tailed (left) and Marbled Godwit at Port Renfrew

■ *Godwits* - Godwits are large shorebirds with distinctive long, upturned bills. Three species have been reported on Vancouver Island during the spring and fall migrations: Marbled, Bar-tailed, and Hudsonian. Marbled Godwits are the largest with an average length of 45 cm. The Bar-tailed is next at 40 cm and the Hudsonian is smallest at 39 cm. Chances of seeing a Bar-tailed or Hudsonian are quite rare while the Marbled is a regular visitor during the spring and fall.

Bar-tailed Godwits nest in Europe, Asia, and Alaska. Most winter in south-east Asia, Australia, and New Zealand. It was a rare treat for birders as a Bar-tailed Godwit stayed at Port Renfrew for most of September, 2006.

Bar-tailed Godwit at Port Renfrew

Marbled Godwit at Cattle Point

Marbled Godwits breed in the southern regions of the prairie provinces then disperse east and west to the Atlantic and Pacific coastlines. They are commonly seen on Vancouver Island during the spring and fall migrations. It is not unusual to see them with the Whimbrels on Victoria Golf Course in the spring.

Ruddy Turnstone at Clover Point

Surfbird at Clover Point

■ Rockpipers is a term used to describe shorebirds that are usually found foraging along the rocky shorelines of the west coast. The Rock Sandpiper, Surf Bird, Black Turnstone, and Ruddy Turnstone are four rockpipers that I was fortunate to photograph. My many attempts to find the Wandering Tattler at Ogden Point all ended in disappointment, but there's always next year.

The Black Turnstone is the most common and abundant rockpiper on Vancouver Island. A large wintering population inhabits the rocky coastline from early August to late April. Ogden, Clover, and Cattle Points are all excellent places to see Black Turnstones in the Victoria region. Columbia Beach and Qualicum are good venues up Island. When breeding season arrives, the Black Turnstones head for the coastal regions of Alaska where they mate with the same partner year after year. Both parents incubate the four eggs and both tend to the young.

Ruddy Turnstones are widespread around the world as they winter on every continent except Antarctica. On North America most of them winter on the coastlines of the U.S., Mexico, and Central America. A few are believed to winter on Tree Island near Comox. Otherwise, only a few are seen on Vancouver Island during migration stopovers to and from the Arctic coast.

Surfbirds and Rock Sandpipers both winter on Vancouver Island. Surfbirds are more common and usually seen in flocks while the Rock Sandpiper tends to be a loner mixed in with other rockpipers.

Rock Sandpiper at Whiffin Spit

Black Turnstones at Admiral's Lagoon

■ *Shady Character* - *Despite measuring 45 cm (18 in), the solitary Green Heron is seldom seen as it lurks in the shadows of the tall vegetation in marshes and beside streams. Like all herons, it utilizes stealth, patience , and a quick bill to snatch unsuspecting prey like small fish, crustaceans, insects, and snakes. Green Herons breed on V.I. but winter in southern U.S. and Mexico.*

Green Heron at Port Alberni

■ The Whimbrel is another large shorebird that stops on Vancouver Island during migration. It is a common sight at the Victoria Golf Course every spring. It nests in the Arctic and winters along the Pacific coast from southern Oregon to the tip of South America.

Whimbrel at the Victoria Golf Course

■ The cryptically patterned Wilson's Snipe blends in so well with the vegetation that it is usually not seen until it is flushed. It is a short-distance migrant, and a few do winter on Vancouver Island.

Wilson's Snipe at the Courtenay Airpark

■ *Driving Range Bird* - Cattle Egrets are small herons that are uncommon on Vancouver Island, but one or two seem to be reported every year. They are usually found in farm fields near livestock where they feed on insects stirred up by the animals. They winter in southern California, coastal Texas, Florida and further south. In the fall of 2005, a Cattle Egret spent a week at the Fun Pacific Golf centre in Duncan dodging golf balls and foraging for worms.

Cattle Egret at Fun Pacific Golf Driving Range (Duncan)

■ *Air Miles? - The American-Golden-Plover is a powerful long-distance flier that breeds in the high Arctic tundra of Canada and Alaska and winters in South America. Only a few are seen on Vancouver Island. The most likely time is during the fall migration.*

American Golden Plover at Holden Creek

3 Lesser Yellowlegs and 2 Stilt Sandpipers at Holden Creek

Stilt Sandpiper looking for a spot to start probing for insects and invertebrates

■ *Year of the Stilt - 2005 was definitely the year of the Stilt for Vancouver Island as unprecedented numbers appeared in the fall migration. Normally, one or two a year are reported, but 15 - 20 were seen at Holden Creek for about a week in mid-August. Their migration from the Arctic coast usually heads down central and eastern Canada on the way to South America.*

Greater Yellowlegs at Admiral's Lagoon hustling after a small fish.

▲ The Greater Yellowlegs is a long-distance migrant. Some travel from as far as South America to nest in Alaska and the northern half of the provinces.

▼ All Shook Up - Looking like a feather duster is all part of the regular and necessary grooming routine for the Short-billed Dowitcher.

Short-billed Dowitcher at Holden Creek

Pectoral Sandpiper at Holden Creek

▲ On the Prowl - Small numbers of Pectoral Sandpipers stop on Vancouver Island during the fall migration to South America from the Arctic coast.

▼ A Dapper Plover - Semipalmated Plovers are regular visitors to Vancouver Island on their migration stopover to the U.S. and Mexico from the Arctic.

Semipalmated Plover at Holden Creek

Westerns Prefer the West - Most Western Sandpipers migrate from Alaska along the west coast to the Pacific and Atlantic coasts of the U.S. and Mexico.

Western Sandpiper at Oyster Bay

Least But Not Last - The Least Sandpiper might be the smallest peep, but it is also one of the most abundant to visit Vancouver Island during the spring and fall migrations.

Least Sandpiper at Kaye Road

My Favorite Peep - The first peep I ever photographed was a Semipalmated Sandpiper. They're not as common as other peeps as most of them migrate to South America via the central and Atlantic flyways.

Semipalmated Sandpiper at Holden Creek

All-World Bird - Sanderlings are small sandpipers seen on beaches and shorelines all over the world. They breed in the Arctic and winter along temperate and tropical coastlines.

Sanderling at Admiral's Lagoon

Spotted Sandpiper at River's Edge

■ *Naughty Spottie* - Spotted Sandpipers are widespread across North America. Their breeding range is vast, extending from the mid-south of United States to the Arctic coast of Canada and Alaska. They winter from the southern states down through Mexico, Central America, and South America. Female Spotted Sandpipers arrive at their breeding sites first to establish their territory and prepare the nests. But after mating, their model behavior deteriorates as they leave the males with the chick-rearing chores and take up with another mate. This promiscuous scenario is often repeated several times. On Vancouver Island Spotted Sandpipers are common from salt water beaches and fresh water ponds to alpine areas like Bear Mountain and Paradise Meadows. Some even stay around for the Christmas Bird Counts.

Spotted Sandpiper chick at River's Edge

28

nesting Killdeer at Springford's Farm (Nanoose)

■ *Model Family* - Unlike the Spotted Sandpipers, the Killdeer are models of moral behavior. Both males and females share in nest preparation, chick-rearing, and protection. The nest is a shallow scrape in an open field, farmyard, parking lot, shoreline, or even on the roadside. Four stone coloured eggs are laid and incubation is shared by both parents. In the event of danger, the parents utilize the broken wing display to lure the predator from the nest. However, this strategy is of little use if the danger comes from a farm tractor or lawn equipment. Despite the hazards of civilization, Killdeer have successfully adapted to human modified environments. Their willingness to nest close to human activity and ability to raise more than one brood have made them the most widespread and abundant of the American plovers.

Killdeer nest at Springford's

Baby Killdeer at Cassidy Airport

Deep Bay

The wind could be howling at Qualicum, but Deep Bay and Baynes Sound would be a sheet of glass disturbed only by the ripples of ducks, grebes, loons, and other seabirds. It is a special place not just for the birds, but also for those who wish to enjoy the birds. It is the best place on Vancouver Island for close-up looks at Long-tailed Ducks and many other sea birds as well as the occasional songbird.

Water Birds

male Long-tailed Duck at Deep Bay

◉ *Rubber Duckies* - Wouldn't it be cute to have Buffleheads in your bathtub? They are the smallest North American duck and common on fresh and salt water but not usually seen on land during the winter. I have only seen two on land in my four years of birding. It was reassuring to see that they actually have legs. During the nesting season they migrate nocturnally to small ponds and lakes of the boreal forest in central and northern Canada. The females claim unused Northern Flicker holes for their nests and lay about 9 eggs. They incubate the eggs, raise the ducklings, and return to their coastal winter habitat in late October and November.

male Bufflehead at Qualicum

female Bufflehead at Deep Bay

male Harlequin Duck at Qualicum

■ *Art Nouveau* - *Picasso would be proud of the artistic rendering of male Harlequin Ducks. The rich chestnut flanks and bold white markings on slate gray bodies is a work of art for all to enjoy. They are common along the rocky shorelines of the Pacific coast where they frolic in turbulent waters and dive for* *mollusks and crustaceans. As short-distance migrants, Harlequins follow streams and rivers up to the mountains to nest in well-concealed crevices or tree cavities. The females lay 5 - 7 eggs, incubate for about 4 weeks, rear the ducklings for a few more weeks and return to the coast by late August and September.*

female Wood Duck at King's Pond

■ *People's Choice - It's unanimous. Wood Ducks are the most beautiful ducks on the Island and maybe the continent. They are medium-sized fresh water ducks found in wooded swamps and ponds. Although usually wary of people, they can become quite domesticated in parks or ponds where ducks are regularly fed. King's Pond in Saanich is a good example where Wood Ducks readily join in the feeding frenzy with the Mallards, Ring-necked Ducks, and Lesser Scaups.*

male Wood Duck at King's Pond

The Redhead is a medium-sized diving duck that breeds from the prairies to Alaska. Its winter range is primarily the southern states, Mexico, and the Caribbean. Only a few are lucky enough to winter on Vancouver Island.

Male Redhead Duck at King's Pond

Big Bill - The over-sized bill of the Northern Shoveler is equipped with fine comb-like projections to filter out food from the mud and water dredged from the bottom of shallow ponds.

Male Northern Shoveler at Somenos Marsh

Cow Duck? - The Female Redhead is the Cowbird of the duck world. She is known to lay her eggs in the nests of many other duck species as well as the American Bittern and even the Northern Harrier.

Female Redhead at the Ridge Golf Course

International Duck - Greater Scaups are common to Eurasia as well as North America. They breed in northern Canada and Alaska and winter along the Pacific and Atlantic coasts.

Male Greater Scaup at Parksville Beach

▼ American Wigeons are the most abundant ducks in the Pacific Northwest despite large population losses in the 1980's because of prairie drought. Populations have recovered, and they are now widespread across North America. They breed inland throughout Canada and Alaska and winter along the Pacific and Atlantic coasts down to northern South America. They are medium-sized dabbling ducks, and their powerful short bills are suited for tearing vegetation not just in the water but also on land. It is not uncommon to see large flocks dabbling in estuaries or marshes or grazing on grassy fields like the fairways of Fairwinds Golf Course.

male Eurasian Wigeon at French Creek

"Ain't she sweet!"
female American Wigeon
at French Creek

female Eurasian Wigeon at French Creek

◀ *The Immigrant - In every large flock of American Wigeons there always seems to be a few handsome red-headed strangers - male Eurasian Wigeons. Eurasians are common and widespread in Europe and Asia, but they are uncommon in North America. Most North American visitors are believed to migrate from Siberia and Iceland. In fact, there are more Eurasians than meet the eye as the females are very similar to their American Wigeon counterparts and often overlooked. Female Eurasians are lighter and warmer in colour. The differences are quite subtle and only obvious to experienced birders.*

male American Wigeon at French Creek

■ *The Scoop on the Scaup - Unlike the Greater Scaups, the Lesser Scaups are mainly a North American bird. In fact, they are the most abundant duck in North America. Although they seem to prefer fresh water, they are also regularly seen in salt water. Their breeding range extends from central and western Canada up to Alaska. They winter from Vancouver Island south to Mexico and Central America. They are a diving duck, and their ducklings are able to dive from the day they are hatched. Their diet consists of clams, snails, aquatic insects, seeds, and aquatic plants.*

female Lesser Scaup at Fairwinds

male Lesser Scaup at Deep Bay

male Ring-necked Duck at King's Pond
(Notice the faint ring on the neck?)

female Ring-necked Duck at Fairwinds

◀▲ *Where's the Ring? - It looks like a ring on the bills, but where's the ring on the necks of the Ring-necked Ducks? Unless their necks are extended and the light is at the right angle, the purplish ring on the necks is usually imperceptible. But with the bump or peak at the back of the head and the ring on the bill, they are very common and easy to identify. Their usual habitat is in fresh water ponds during the winter all over Vancouver Island and south as far as Central America and the Caribbean. Their nesting range is from the interior of B.C. across to the east coast.*

41

female Common Merganser and ducklings
at the Englishman River estuary

▲ *Ducky Day Care* - 18 red-headed ducklings! That's how many I saw at the Englishman River in 2004. That's a lot for any parent, but the female Common Merganser is capable of laying up to 18 eggs. Another possibility is that two families have been combined. Apparently, the females are territorial and when two families collide, the loser loses the territory and the family. Common Mergansers nest across Canada and up to Alaska. Their winter range extends along the Pacific coast to most of the U.S. It also extends to Eurasia and northern Africa and northern Vietnam. Their diet consists of fish, mollusks, crustaceans, amphibians, worms, small mammals, and insects.

male Common Merganser at Art Mann Park

► Green-winged Teal are the smallest and one of the most abundant dabbling ducks on Vancouver Island. Their favorite habitat is tidal mud flats where they probe for seeds, sedges, and vegetation. They also frequent shallow marshes, estuaries, and flooded fields. Their breeding range extends across Canada from the interior of B.C. and includes much of northern Canada and Alaska. The females usually lay 8 - 9 eggs and incubate and raise the families on their own while the males disappear for their molting. During the winter their range extends from the coast of B.C. to the southern two-thirds of the U.S., all of Mexico, and the Caribbean.

female Green-winged Teal at San Pariel

male Green-winged Teal at San Pariel

female Barrow's Goldeneye at Parksville Bay

male Barrow's Goldeneye at Parksville Bay

■ *Sex on the Bay* - Procreation is the most beautiful act in life for without it, there would be no life. The calm water and blue sky at Parksville Bay early last spring was the perfect setting for nature's most precious one act play.

The first step for birds to mate is to find a mate. There are many techniques used by male birds to attract a female. Peacocks and birds of Paradise display their gorgeous tail feathers; Mockingbirds and Robins sing into the night; and hummingbirds perform swooping flights. Ducks like the Common and Barrow's Goldeneye use head throws, wing flapping, upward stretches, and crest raisings.

After the pair bond is formed there are a series of pre-copulatory activities. The female simply lies prone in the water while the male incites her with techniques such as water twitching, preening behind the wing, steaming towards the female, or displaying the jewels.

Finally the male mounts the female and the transfer of sperm takes place. I'm not sure why the male lifts the head of the female, but it seems logical to prevent her from drowning or the discomfort of being submerged. The position is maintained for about a minute, and then it is over. The marriage is consummated, and the honeymoon is booked for some five star tree cavity in the interior of B.C., Yukon, or Alaska.

On the breeding grounds the female tries to find her own tree cavity and lays from 1 to 12 eggs. If nest sites are unavailable, she will simply lay them in another duck's nest and let the other unsuspecting duck raise the family.

45

female Red-breasted Merganser at Deep Bay

■ Red-breasted Mergansers are large diving ducks that breed across northern Canada and Alaska. In winter they disperse to Pacific coastal areas from Alaska to Mexico and similarly from Newfoundland to Mexico on the Atlantic coast. They also disperse to southern Europe and China. They are usually found on large lakes, rivers, and salt water. Like the other Mergansers they are powerful divers and feed on fish, crustaceans, insects, and tadpoles.

male Red-breasted Merganser at Deep Bay

■ *Nike Bird - I don't think that White-winged Scoters have the same endorsement contract as Tiger Woods. That's why they wear the "swoosh" backwards. One of their favorite foods is the invasive varnish clam which seems to be abundant in local waters.*

male White-winged Scoter at Qualicum

■ *Gadwall are common dabbling ducks that winter on Vancouver Island, the southern half of United States, and Mexico. They breed in the prairie heartland of Canada and United States. They are common at Buttertubs and Somenos during the winter.*

male and female Gadwall at Elk Lake

■ *Hooded Mergansers are year-round residents of Vancouver Island. They are the smallest of the three local mergansers, and usually found in shallow freshwater ponds where they dive for fish, crabs, crayfish, and other seafood delicacies.*

male Hooded Merganser at Oak Bay

48

female Black Scoter at Qualicum

■ A Brown Black Scoter - Half of the Black Scoters aren't black because they are females. Black Scoters are the least abundant of the local scoters. Their populations seem stable but they are under constant threat from oil pollution and heavy metal contamination.

Blue-winged Teal and Green-winged Teal at San Malo

■ A Teal With Appeal - Blue-winged Teals have been known to nest on Vancouver Island in the past, but they are now seen only during migration in the spring and fall. They breed from the interior of B.C. to the prairie provinces.

female Surf Scoter at Qualicum

■ Like most female ducks, the female Surf Scoter lacks the fancy colours or structures of the male. The reason, of course, is survival. The female must try to remain as inconspicuous as possible especially when she is raising a brood of ducklings.

49

■ *Mellow Yellow* - *Yellow-billed Loons are the largest of the loons and easily identified by their bright yellowish bills. They nest around tundra lakes near the Arctic coast from Hudson's Bay to Alaska. Their normal winter range is along the Pacific coast from Alaska to Vancouver Island. However, a few are sun-seekers and have been known to show up at vacation locations like southern California, Arizona, and Texas. Around Vancouver Island they are usually seen as individuals or in the company of Common Loons.*

Yellow-billed Loon at Deep Bay

Eared Grebe at
River's Edge

▲ Fresh Water Surprise - Eared Grebes are the most abundant grebe in the world. They are normally seen in salt water around Vancouver Island. It was a surprise to find one in a feshwater pond on Rascal Lane Pond during the fall of 2005.

▶ Kiss My Butt Bird? - Rumor has it that the native name for Marbled Murrelets is just a little more graphic than the title above in reference to the part of the anatomy most frequently displayed by the bird. Marbled Murrelets nest in old growth forests along the coast.

▶ Restaurant Bird? - The Rhinoceros Auklet is a sea bird, but food can throw caution out the window. Such was the case at Ogden Point when I watched an Auklet taxi cautiously almost up to the restaurant to corral a small school of fish.

Marbled Murrelet at Deep Bay

Rhinoceros Auklet at Ogden Point

Horned Grebe at Deep Bay

Tufted Puffin
near Tofino

Western Grebe at
Comox Marina

▲ Ready for Romance - After a winter in dull gray, black, and white, the Horned Grebe is dressed in its finest breeding colours to impress its mate. Horned Grebes nest inland from the interior of B.C. across Canada to Ontario and north into Alaska.

◄ Popular Puffin - The colourful and endearing Tufted Puffins are usually found off the west coast of Vancouver Island. They nest on rocky islets and isolated islands where they can find some soil to excavate for nest burrows.

◄ Graceful Grebe - Huge flocks of Western Grebes used to be common around Vancouver Island, but that is thing of the past. On a Christmas Bird Count at Deep Bay around 1980, 15, 174 Western Grebes were reported.

American Coot at Buttertubs Marsh

◄► An Imitation Duck - It swims like a duck and dives like a duck, but it isn't a duck. Just look at its unducklike feet and bill. It's an American Coot commonly found with ducks in marshy ponds and swamps like Rithet's Bog or Buttertubs Marsh.

◄ The Secretive Sora - The Sora is one of the most common and widely distributed rails in North America, but it is seldom seen. It isn't really a water bird but it is always found around water. It is a secretive inhabitant of freshwater swamps and marshes and lurks in the bulrushes and marsh vegetation foraging for seeds and aquatic invertebrates. The Sora breeds from northern Canada to the northern half of the U.S. It winters in the southern states, Mexico, Caribbean, Central America, and northern South America.

Sora at Buttertubs Marsh

American Coot at Rithet's Bog

"Fonzie," the Double-crested
Cormorant at French Creek

Pelagic Cormorants at Chrome Island

Brandt's Cormorant at Chrome Island

■ *Fisher Birds* - Cormorants are large, dark sea birds with long, flexible necks and short, rounded wings. They have large webbed feet and non-buoyant feathers which are adaptations for fast underwater swimming. They are expert fishing birds, and that fact was not lost to fishermen in China and Japan who used cormorants for commercial fishing. Modern methods have mostly replaced cormorant fishing, but the tradition called "ukai" is still practiced in Japan. Because their wings are not water-proof, cormorants are commonly seen with their wings outstretched to dry.

Double-crested, Brandt's, and Pelagic are the three cormorant species commonly found around Vancouver Island. The Red-faced Cormorant is a rare visitor from Alaska and the Aleutian Islands.

Double-crested Cormorants are the most wide-spread and found all across the continent in salt and fresh water. They have thicker and lighter coloured bills than other cormorants, yellow faces at the base of their bills, and distinctive kinked necks when in flight. The double crests are seen on adults only during the breeding season. Breeding colonies are found on offshore islets like Mandarte and Chain Islands near Victoria.

Tan cheek patches identify the Brandt's Cormorants. They are found along the rocky shoreline of the Pacific. They can dive up to 150 feet for fish, shrimp, or crabs.

Pelagic Cormorants are the smallest of the three species. White rump patches are a distinguishing feature of breeding adults. They feed mainly on non-commercial fish, crustaceans, and small marine animals.

57

■ *Tern Time* - *Two species of terns are commonly seen around Vancouver Island. During the spring and summer, small groups of Caspian Terns show up along the coastline. They are conspicuous with their large carrot-sized orange bills.*

At the end of August and early September, Common Terns stop, rest, and feed at Deep Bay during their fall migration en route to South America. Their breeding range extends from Alberta east to Newfoundland. Their longish orange bills with black tips distinguish them from the similar Arctic Tern.

Caspian Tern at Chesterman Beach (Tofino)

Common Tern at Deep Bay

58

Red Phalarope at Whiffin Spit (Sooke)

◀ *Christmas Surprise - Red Phalaropes are normally out at sea during the winter, but after a series of big storms in December 2005, they began showing up close to shore along the west coast from Oregon to Vancouver Island. Some were even found inland at Somenos Marsh and Langford Lake.*

Common Tern at Deep Bay

■ *Gull Identification?* - *Gulls are often problematic when it comes to identification. Not only are there many species, but there are many plumage changes before a gull matures. Add into the mixture a lot of hybridization and the adjective "confusing" is an understatement. However, if you can get past the "garbage dump" stereotyping, gulls are interesting, and to some they are fascinating.*

Beginners should only focus on the adults. First, look at the legs. Are they pink or yellow? If they are pink, think Glaucous-winged, Western, Thayer's, Herring or Glaucous Gull. If they are yellow, they might be California, Ring-billed, or Mew Gulls.

If you are interested, a good guide book is required, and it won't take long to master some of the more common gulls.

There are also many uncommon gulls that visit Vancouver Island. A Slaty-backed Gull was reported in Parksville in the spring of '06 and another at Cattle Point in the fall of '06. Other gulls reported in the past few years include the Franklin's, Sabine's, and Little Gull.

Two common gulls not mentioned yet are the Heermann's with its distinctive orange bill and the Bonaparte's with its black head and orange legs. The Heermann's is common on the south and west coasts.

Gull identification is definitely a challenge, but it is part of the fun of birding.

Mew Gulls at Campbell River

Thayer's Gull
at Qualicum

■ The Thayer's Gull is common around Vancouver Island during the winter. At 58 cm (23 in) in length, it is just smaller than the abundant Glaucous-winged Gull. The distinguishing features for the adult are pink legs, black wing-tips, round head, purplish orbital ring, and smallish bill. Its breeding range is on Arctic coast and Arctic islands of Canada.

■ The Herring Gull is a large gull that is widespread across North America, but only small numbers occur on Vancouver Island. With pink legs and black wing-tips, the adult looks like any gull, but experienced birders will notice a very pale yellow iris and a relatively pale gray back. The non-breeding adult has a extensively streaked head while the breeding adult has a clear white head.

Herring Gull at French Creek

■ The largest and palest gull one is likely to see on V.I. is the Glaucous Gull. It is fairly easy to identify because of its white wing tips. With an average length of 67 cm, it is slightly larger than the common Glaucous-winged and Western Gulls. It breeds on the Arctic coast of Canada and Alaska and prefers to winter in northern waters. A few are always found on Vancouver Island.

Glaucous Gull at French Creek

■ The Ring-billed is a medium-sized gull. It has yellow legs and eyes, and a red eye ring. It is more common inland than along the coast. Small numbers are seen regularly on Vancouver Island. It is found around landfills, parks, golf courses, farm fields, and coastal beaches where it feeds on fish, insects, earthworms, and garbage. It breeds in southern Canada from the interior of B.C. to the east coast.

Ring-billed Gulls at Admiral's Lagoon

■ A Buttertubs Ballad

There are many stories at Buttertubs
Marsh
Some are sweet and some are harsh
Peter Pied-billed was in love
Paula he was dreaming of
Promised her the finest nest
Always to love her the very best
To honor and obey 'til death do us part
To love and cherish with all his heart

One day a stranger came to town
And boldly threw the challenge down
The law of the marsh was known to all
Peter was ready to meet the call
The battle was fierce
The battle was rough
But finally the stranger
Had enough

The stranger turned and ran
Which wasn't in his plan
Peter had bravely met the test
Survival of the very best
Paula had cheered her hero on
And was glad the stranger was gone
She was happy and beamed with pride
She wanted Peter at her side

Like many stories at the marsh
Some are sweet and some are harsh
Peter was a hero in Paula's eyes
And she wasn't going to apologize
For the best reward she could think of
Was to give Peter all her love.

(My apologies to all poets on Vancouver
Island. Peter and Paula were the proud
parents of three candy-striped baby Pied-
billed Grebes.)

Bonaparte's Gulls are small gulls common on Vancouver Island for a few weeks in the spring during their migration stopover to north-central Canada or Alaska. They are even more common on their return as they linger from July to late fall before heading for the Washington coast and as far south as Mexico and the Caribbean.

▲ adult breeding Bonaparte's Gull

juvenile Bonaparte's Gull at Deep Bay

Brant Time - Coinciding with the herring spawn in late February and early March, massive flocks of Brant, gulls, and ducks congregate in record numbers from Comox to Nanoose. It is one of the major natural events on Vancouver Island as thousands of migrating Brant stop to fatten up on eel grass and the bounty of herring roe; flotillas of ducks as far as the eye can see gorge themselves with floating roe; and blankets of gulls cover the beaches like new-fallen snow. Although the spawn is over in a week, the feeding frenzy for the birds continues for several weeks until they are ready to head for their distant breeding grounds.

Brant and Mew Gulls at Admiral's Lagoon

The Real Blue Jay - Blue Jays are common in central and eastern Canada, but only 1 or 2 a year make it to Vancouver Island. They adapt easily to urban and sub-urban areas, and readily visit backyard feeders. Their habits are very similar to Steller's Jays as they stash seeds and nuts for future use. The Steller's Jay and the Blue Jay are the only two jays with crests.

Blue Jay in Melodee Mole's backyard, North Saanich

Forest & Field Birds

◄ juvenile Gray Jay and
▼ adult Gray Jay at Mt. Washington

Mountain Birds- Gray Jays or Whiskey Jacks are found at higher elevations where they live year-round. If you're ever skiing or hiking on Mt. Washington, make sure you take some extra bread as these fearless jays will eat right out of your hand. Like other jays, they stash their food and save it for leaner times. They are known to cement food to trees with their own saliva.

Steller's Jay at Dolphin Lake

Provincial Bird - Despite it's designation as the provincial emblem, the Steller's Jay's boisterous and raucous behavior is not always as dignified as it should be. It often monopolizes backyard feeders much to the chagrin of smaller birds, and pilfers more than its share of seed. Steller's Jays summer at higher elevations and return to coastal regions for the winter.

■ *Duck Bird?* - *The American Dipper is part song bird and part duck. Like a song bird, it can often be found perched and singing on a branch or rock. When it decides to eat, it behaves more like a duck. It wades, runs, and swims in the shallow waters of its resident stream and reaches or dives under to catch its prey. Its diet consists of fish eggs, aquatic larvae, small fish, and insects such as mayflies, stone flies, or caddis flies. Nest sites are often found behind waterfalls, in streamside crevices, or under man-made bridges. Cold weather is not a problem for the hardy American Dipper. It can endure the coldest winters and only moves when its stream freezes over. Goldstream Park is one of the best places to observe American Dippers, but they can also be found in many other Island streams and rivers.*

American Dipper at Goldstream Park

female Belted Kingfisher
at Comox

male Belted Kingfisher
at French Creek

■ The Fisher King - Solitary, patient, and dynamic, the Belted Kingfisher is a marvellous hunter as it transforms into a feathered spear and plunges into the water to grasp its slippery prey. The male is blue and white with u blue chest band. The female is the same with the addition of an orange waist band. Adults get together at breeding time and nest in long burrows dug into the sand or soil of a cliff or bank

male Belted Kingfisher at French Creek

*juvenile Northern Shrike
at Nanoose Estuary*

■ *A Sinister Songbird* - *Despite their small size and angelic demeanor, Northern Shrikes are predators, and males are known to skewer smaller birds on thorn bushes or barbed wire to impress the females. This practice is also a way of storing food for future use. Without the talons or size of a raptor, Northern Shrikes rely on speed and powerful bills to catch and dispatch their prey. Besides small birds, they enjoy dining on mice, moles, crickets, grasshoppers, and other large insects.*

Northern Shrikes are migratory and spend their summers in northern B.C., Yukon, and Alaska. They are common on Vancouver Island for the winter and are usually found in open or semi-open habitats like fields, shorelines, and estuaries. Their winter range is primarily southern Canada and the northern half of the U.S.

■ *Kestrel Time -* *For the past three years I have kept a vigil during the first two weeks of June for the Kaye Road American Kestrels to fledge. I have been lucky to find them every year. They only stay around for about two days so it's a narrow window of opportunity to enjoy them. They are considered one of the most colourful raptors in the world. Their breeding range extends across Canada and into Alaska. They are scarce in the winter as Vancouver Island is at the northern edge of the American Kestrels' winter range.*

juvenile American Kestrel at Kaye Road

◄ adult male American Kestral

Cooper's Hawk at
Fairwinds

■ *A Snowy Year* - *The winter of '05 was an exceptional year as large numbers of Snowy Owls appeared in the Pacific Northwest. Some speculate that it was the result of a very successful breeding year. At least a dozen were reported on Vancouver Island, and at Boundary Bay on the mainland, 15 - 20 birds were present all winter.*

Snowy Owl at Nanaimo River Estuary

Barred Owl at Buttertubs Marsh

■ *Shakespeare's Bird? - The Barred probably wasn't Shakespeare's bird, but it is becoming more prominent on Vancouver Island. The Barred averages 53 cm in length compared to 56 cm for the Great Horned Owl. However, the Great Horned is almost twice as heavy and much more powerful. The Barred knows enough to avoid the Great Horned when their territories overlap.*

recently fledged Great Horned Owl at Rathtrevor Park

young Great Horned
Owl at Kaye Road

◄▲ *Fuzzy-Wuzzies - They look cute and cuddly with their feathered ear tufts, but it won't be long before they are formidable hunters like adult Great Horned Owls. With tiny baffles on the front of their wings, they are able to swoop silently to snatch unsuspecting prey such as rats, rabbits, amphibians, cats, crows, and even skunks. Great Horned Owls are non-migratory and start nesting in January. Up to 4 eggs are laid and incubated for 5 weeks. Babies are able to fly quite well in about 10 weeks after hatching.*

► *Short-eared Owls are migratory and move north or inland to central and northern Canada and Alaska to nest. They winter on Vancouver Island and as far south as South America. Their favorite habitats are fields, meadows, marshes, and shorelines where they search for voles, mice, reptiles, small birds, rabbits and other prey.*

Short-eared Owls at
Nanaimo Estuary

■ *2005 Bird of the Year* - On Oct. 7/05 *Ralph Hocken of Lantzville discovered an interesting bird at Columbia Beach. Local bird expert, Guy Monty, was astounded when he saw the photo and identified it as a Northern Wheatear. According to unofficial sources, the last one reported on Vancouver Island was around 1970 at the Victoria Airport. The Wheatear was a twitcher's delight as it stayed around for almost two weeks allowing fabulous close-up views to over 400 birders from all over B.C. Wheatears breed in the Yukon and Alaska, but their migration is normally to Asia and Africa. Only a rare individual migrates south to Canada and U.S. The Wheatear is a small bird about 14 cm (5.5 in) in length. It actively forages on the ground for grasshoppers, bugs, and large insects. By general consensus of Island birders, the Northern Wheatear was indeed the "2005 Bird of the Year." Apparently "wheat" and "ear" have nothing to do with the bird's name - it's simply a sanitized version of "white arse." which is a very appropriate description.*

looking for the next meal

Northern Wheatear
enjoying a snack

time to relax

Northern Wheatear at Columbia Beach

■ *Coming Up Rosy-Finch* - *Normally when you're truant from your chores you don't get rewarded, but occasionally there are exceptions. Such was the case on Oct. 20/06 when Joachim Ruhstein tempted me to skip my chores and go to Victoria for some birding. I thought I was paying the price for truancy with overcast skies and being skunked at Clover and Cattle Point, but on our return to Clover Point, the sun broke through, and we came up "Gray-crowned Rosy-Finch." It was the first in the Victoria checklist area since 1996 at Whiffin Spit. The Rosy-Finch is believed to nest on the mountains of Strathcona Park, but it is seldom seen at sea level.*

Gray-crowned Rosy-Finch at Clover Point

84

■ *Savannah Sparrows are abundant on Vancouver Island and most of Canada and Alaska during the spring and summer. They are found around airports, agricultural fields, grassy meadows, estuaries, and shorelines where they forage for insects, insect larvae, and seeds. Their winter range includes southern U.S., Mexico, and Central America.*

Savannah Sparrow at China Beach

■ *Vanishing Vesper - In Canada the Vesper Sparrow breeds from the interior of B.C. to the Maritimes, but there is also a coastal subspecies on Vancouver Island that is endangered. Only a few breeding pairs exist, and they are all at the Cassidy Airport. Their habitat and breeding success is being monitored by the Nanaimo Area land Trust.*

Vesper Sparrow at Cassidy Airport

Ted's Birds - Thanks to Ted Ardley for sharing his Saanich backyard and the White-throated and Clay-coloured Sparrows.

A few White-throated Sparrows are seen regularly during the fall and winter on Vancouver Island which is not surprising as part of their winter range extends down the Pacific coast from Washington.

White-throated Sparrow in Saanich

It is a rare treat to see a Clay-coloured Sparrow on Vancouver Island as its breeding range extends from central B.C. east to Saskatchewan. Its winter range is primarily around Mexico

Clay-coloured Sparrow in Saanich

Painted Bunting at Brentwood Bay

◀ *Howdy Pardner!* - One would hardly expect a Texas bird to be visiting Vancouver Island in the spring but that's exactly what happened at Brentwood Bay. On March 24, 2006, Jeremy Gaaten was surprised to see a wayward Painted Bunting at his feeders. It was the first Painted Bunting ever reported on Vancouver Island. The southern tourist enjoyed Jeremy's hospitality until it flew off into the sunset on April 4.

◀ *Winter Treat* - Often referred to as "snowbirds," Snow Buntings are pretty songbirds that nest in the high Arctic and winter in southern Canada and northern U.S. Large flocks are seen on the open grasslands of eastern Washington, but sightings on Vancouver Island are only occasional. Cattle and Clover Points in Victoria are the most common locations for birds to be reported. My only sighting has been at Deep Bay on November 3, 2005.

Snow Bunting at Deep Bay

The male Snow Bunting is very hardy and returns to the rocky Arctic tundra to stake out its nesting territory in early April when snow still covers the ground and temperatures often plummet to minus thirty. The sensible female follows in five or six weeks when the environment is a little more hospitable. A deep crack or crevice in a rock face or boulder field is chosen for the nest site. It is lined with lichens, roots, grass, feathers, and fur to keep the nest and nestlings warm. The female lays and incubates 2 - 7 eggs while the male is busy providing the food.

Snow Buntings forage by walking around. Their diet consists of weeds, seeds, and insects.

Western Meadowlark at Cattle Point

◀ Western Meadowlarks are attractive robin-sized birds found around open grasslands, estuaries, and agricultural fields during the fall and winter on Vancouver Island. In early spring they migrate inland to the interior of B.C. for the breeding season. The innocent looking males usually mate with two females.

▼ Horned Larks are the only native species of the lark family in North America. They love open country and prefer bare ground to grassy fields. Their diet consists mainly of grass and weed seeds, but they feed insects to their young. They are seen occasionally on Vancouver Island primarily in the fall at open areas like Clover Point, Ship's Point and Deep Bay Spit.

Horned Lark at Deep Bay

■ *The Gray Ghost* - *The long, slim Townsend's Solitaires seem to materialize out of nothing as they traverse Vancouver Island on the way to their mountainous nesting grounds in B.C., Yukon, and Alaska. Most sightings occur during the spring migration when they stop to feed on spiders, insects, and berries. Very few birds are seen during the winter although southern Vancouver Island is included as part of their winter range which extends down to Mexico. The Townsend's Solitaires nest on the ground and if possible, on cut banks where some overhead protection is available. At their winter habitats, their favorite food is juniper berries (cones). Despite their calm disposition, they can become very aggressive and territorial in defending their favorite berry or juniper patch.*

Townsend's Solitaire in my backyard (Na-

90

■ The crossed bills of the Red Crossbills look awkward but are very efficient at prying open fir, spruce, and hemlock cones to harvest the high energy seeds at the base of the cone scales. Since they depend on cones, their main habitat is mature coniferous forests. The only time I have seen them not in a tree was at Nile Creek where they were foraging in a large decaying driftwood log. Presumably, they were after some salt or minerals required for their diet.

Red Crossbill at San Pareil

The Sentry - While Momma and the chicks feed, it is Papa Califor-nia Quail that must keep an eye out for marauding house cats and other predators. (Both photos at San Pariel)

■ *California Cuties* - The only reference I could find about the origins of California Quail on Vancouver Island was on a website journal about an early settler on Whidbey Island. According to the article, after a ship delivered a shipment of California Quail to him around 1850 , it proceeded to Victoria with the other half of the shipment. Regardless of when the quail were introduced, they have been thriving and are generally embraced and enjoyed by most residents. Their habitat is in open areas with lots of dense, brushy cover. They are also found near residential areas where shelter, vegetation, seeds, leaves, and insects are available.

juvenile California Quail at River's Edge

female California Quail at River's Edge

Bread-winner -- With a harem to service and territory to protect , the male Redwing Blackbird has no time for the young or domestic duties. The female is left with the chores of housekeeping and feeding the babies.

Female Redwing
Blackbird at Dolphin Lake

A Heavy Load - The Bald Eagle at Dolphin Lake almost exceeded its load limit. It had to stop and rest before making the next 5 meters to the nest.

Bald Eagle at Dolphin Lake

■ *No Longer Blue* - *Based on behavioral, and DNA differences, in 2006 the AOU reclassified the Blue Grouse into two distinct species. The coastal species is now the Sooty Grouse and the interior species is the Dusky Grouse. Grouse are so confident in their camouflage that they often allow humans and potential predators to walk right up to them. Sensing danger, they can burst into flight if it's not too late to escape. Sooty Grouse are year-round residents on Vancouver Island and found mainly in mountainous regions. The deep, booming call of the male is often heard during the spring.*

juvenile Sooty on the way to Port Renfrew

female Sooty Grouse at Powder Point Road (Nanoose)

► Rock Pigeons are common in urban areas all over the world and were introduced to North America in the early 1600s. They are now common from southern Canada to the southern tip of South America. They are non-migratory.

▼ Ring-necked Pheasants were imported from China to the west coast in the late 1800s as game birds. There are established wild populations primarily on open fields and agricultural grasslands on Vancouver Island, across southern Canada, and throughout northern U.S. Feral populations are sometimes augmented by the introduction of more game birds.

Rock Pigeon at Buttertubs Marsh

Ring-necked Pheasant at Ozero's Farm (Nanoose)

◀ *Downy Wood-peckers are the smallest of the woodpeckers found on Vancouver Island. They are widespread across Canada and the United States. Their average size is 17 cm (6.5 in) in length. They are usually found in mixed deciduous and evergreen forests. Their diet includes insects, arthropods, fruits, seeds, and sap. They are also attracted to suet and seed from backyard feeders.*

▶ *The Hairy Woodpecker looks like an oversized Downy that has been using steroids. It has the same colour and shape but is much larger at 25 cm (9.5 in). It also has a much longer bill in proportion to its head. The Hairy Woodpecker has the same diet as the Downy and also enjoys backyard feeders. Its range is similar but extends further south into Mexico and Central America.*

male Downy Wood-pecker at River's Edge

*male Hairy Woodpecker
in my backyard*

Palm Warbler at Ship's Point

■ Palm Warblers have a distinctive waggle as they bob their tails while foraging for insects, berries, and seeds. They breed in north-central and eastern Canada and usually migrate to southeastern United States and the Caribbean. However, there is also a small wintering population along the Oregon and California coast which probably accounts for some of the strays on Vancouver Island.

Townsend's Warbler at the Notch (Nanoose)

■ Townsend's Warblers nest on Vancouver Island, throughout most of B.C., southern Yukon, and Alaska. A few winter on V.I., but most prefer the warmth further south along the Pacific coast and through Mexico to Central America. They are difficult to photograph as they are often foraging high in the treetops. Their main food consists of insects and honeydew excreted by scale insects.

■ The MacGil-livray's Warbler is a secretive bird that forages along the edges of forests and thickets gleaning insects from low level leaves. It nests from sea level to high elevations throughout B.C. from the Rockies westward and north to southern Yukon. It winters mainly in Mexico and Central America. The eastern counterpart to the MacGillivray's is the Mourning Warbler.

MacGillivray's Warbler at River's Edge

■ Black-throated Gray Warblers have a relatively small geographic range. They nest in southwestern B.C., and western U.S. and winter in Western Mexico. Dry oaks and juniper woods are their favorite habitats, but mixed deciduous and coniferous forests are also frequented. Their favorite foods include insects, inch-worms, and small caterpillars.

Black-throated Gray Warbler in my backyard (Nanoose)

■ *House Calls* - *The cheerful and bouncy House Wrens are a pleasant addition to any location. They are one of most widespread songbirds in North and South America as their breeding range extends from southern Canada to the very southern tip of South America. Their winter range is from southern U.S. to southern South America. They are comfortable in suburban areas and backyards and easily attracted to birdhouses. Vancouver Island is at the northern edge of their summer range, and they are more common from Nanaimo south to Victoria. They are uncommon north of Parksville. In the wild they are usually found in shrubs and trees above the forest floor. Nest-building in the birdhouses or tree cavities begins with the male loading the nest with hundreds of sticks before the female takes over to add the nest cup and lining. The females lay 3 - 10 eggs.*

*House Wren at
River's Edge*

River's Edge

102

Spotted Towhee at
Dolphin Lake

male Purple Finch in
my backyard (Nanoose)

▲ Formerly known as Rufous-sided To-whees, Spotted Towhees are year-round residents on Vancouver Island. They are ground-feeding birds and are often mistaken for larger creatures as they create quite a loud rustling noise while scattering leaves and debris with their double-footed kick in search of food. They are easily attracted to backyard gardens and feeders.

◄ The Raspberry-red male Purple Finches are colourful additions to the avifauna on Vancouver Island where they are enjoyed year-round. They feed on seeds, buds, blossoms, nectar, fruit, and occasionally insects. They get their nectar by crushing the base of flowers. Wild west coast crabapples are one of their favorite treats in the fall. They also enjoy sunflower seeds from backyard feeders.

female Common Yellowthroat at Somenos Marsh

■ *The Lone Ranger - Male Common Yellowthroats are unmistakable with their black masks and colourful bright yellow throats and undersides. Females don't have the mask, but they have the yellow throats and undersides. They are cheerful summer visitors to Vancouver Island where they frequent low brushy areas especially near marshes and wetlands. The females lay 1 - 6 eggs and incubate them while the males provide the females with insects and worms . By late summer and early fall, the Common Yellowthroats migrate back to the southern U.S. , Mexico, and Central America. There are many subspecies of this bird.*

male Common Yellowthroat at River's Edge

juvenile Common Yellowthroat at Nanoose Estuary

■ *Summer Beauty* - Western Tanagers add a touch of tropical beauty to Vancouver Island forests as they migrate from Mexico and Central America to nest in western Canada and United States. Despite their bright colours, they are inconspicuous while they forage in the dense canopy of coniferous forests. The red colour on the male's head is a result of its diet of certain insects.

female Western Tanager at Legacy Marsh

male Western Tanager at Legacy Marsh

■ *Signs of Spring* - The appearance of iridescent blue Tree swallows is a sure sign that spring is around the corner on Vancouver Island. Sometimes they arrive before the insects hatch, but they can survive on seeds and plants. They prefer to nest along shorelines of ponds, swamps, and marshes where they build nests in tree cavities or nest boxes. The nests are lined with feathers and the female lays 2 - 8 eggs. By August it is usually time to migrate south back to the coastal regions of the southern U.S., Mexico, and Central America. An amazing phenomenon to see down south is hundreds of thousands of Tree Swallows at sunset swirling like a huge black cloud before they settle down for their nightly roost in a cattail marsh or swamp.

Tree Swallow at Dolphin Lake

"Where's my food?" cried the juvenile Tree Swallow at San Pariel

"We're hungry too!" screamed the juvenile Barn Swallows at Ogden Point

female Violet-green Swallow at Somenos Marsh

■ Barn Swallows are the most abundant and widespread swallows around the world. They breed across Canada and the U.S. and winter in the southern hemisphere. Originally cave dwellers, they now rely on man-made structures like barns and outbuildings as sites for their mud nests.

■ Violet-green Swallows often arrive on Vancouver Island as early as late February. They are western birds and breed in Alaska, Yukon, B.C. and western U.S. They are cavity nesters and will readily use nest boxes in residential areas. Their winter range includes the southwestern states, Mexico, and Central America.

■ Northern Rough-winged Swallows are aptly named after the rough hooks or barbs on their outer wings. They are cave or cavity nesters and often burrow into sand cliffs like kingfishers. They breed across southern Canada and the U.S. and winter in Mexico and Central America.

■ Cliff Swallows are extremely gregarious and build mud colonies under roofs, bridges, and cliffs. They nest across the U.S. and Canada as far north as Alaska, and they winter in South America.

Northern Rough-winged Swallow at Somenos Marsh

Cliff Swallow by Rene's window (Nanoose)

White-winged Dove
at Beaver Creek Road
(Port Alberni)

◀ *Dandy Dove* - White-winged Doves are residents of south-western U.S. and Mexico where they used to number in the many millions, but extensive land-clearing and hunting took its toll. They are known as tropical doves, and normally winter in Central America and the Caribbean. Occasionally, a wayward bird makes its way to Vancouver Island. During the summer of 2005, a White-winged Dove was visiting Val Geist's feeder in Port Alberni. With Val's kind permission, I was able to sit in his backyard for 2.5 hours to get a few record photos. It was the first White-winged Dove I had ever seen.

Mourning Dove in
Central Saanich

◀ *Wired* - Mourning Doves are common on south Vancouver Island and regularly seen at the bulb fields and other agricultural fields in Saanich. They breed in southern Canada and northern U.S. and are found year-round across the U.S. and Mexico. Despite constant hunting, they are still among the 10 most abundant birds in the U.S. They are difficult to approach when they are on the ground, but they seem more comfortable and approachable when they're on the hydro wires.

Tropical Kingbird
at Dolphin Drive
(Nanoose)

◀ *Tropical Delight* - Tropical Kingbirds are common and widespread in the American tropics. They breed in northern Mexico, southern Texas, and Arizona and then migrate south to Mexico, Central America, and South America. Occasionally, a juvenile or two decides to visit the Pacific Northwest and Vancouver Island. Sightings on Vancouver Island are more prevalent on the west and south coasts. It was a rare treat to see a yellow breasted, robin-sized flycatcher hawking wasps and moths from the trees and hydro lines at and near Fairwinds from Nov. 5 - 8, 2006.

Orange Bishop
at Fairwinds

◄ *Wild or Escaped?* - Was the Orange Bishop at Fairwinds and Garnet and Barb's feeder during the fall of 2006 an escaped cage bird or a vagrant from Africa or California? In Africa the males weave elaborate globe-shaped, hanging nests to attract the females.

▼ *A Winter Guest* - Sandhill Cranes normally winter in south-western U.S. and northern Mexico, but one hardy juvenile enjoyed the wonderful Duncan hospitality so much that it stayed the whole winter (2005 - 06) in a field on Lakes Road. An added benefit was that it had less distance to travel back to its spring breeding grounds in Alaska or northern Canada.

Sandhill Crane at Lakes
Road (Duncan)

► *Jeepers Creeper* - With its cryptic colouration and pattern, the Brown Creeper looks like the bark of a tree until it starts to move. It methodically works it way up the trunk, gleaning insects and bugs with its tweezer-like bill. When it reaches the top, it drops down to the base of another tree and repeats the process.

▼ *Backyard Buddies* - Red-breasted Nuthatches are delightful and friendly birds that readily take advantage of backyard feeders. They also get accustomed to people and will take seed from their hands. In more than one case, they have landed on my camera as I was trying to take their picture.

▼► *The Inconsistent Siskin* - Pine Siskins are known for their irruptive behavior and can appear in huge flocks on Vancouver Island or disappear entirely as they did in 2005. They are often seen on the tops of trees foraging for small seeds, buds, insects, and spiders.

Brown Creeper in my backyard (Nanoose)

Red-breasted Nuthatch in my garden

Pine Siskin near my feeders

Chestnut-backed Chickadee in my backyard

Golden-crowned Kinglet at Fairwinds

Golden-crowned Kinglet at China Beach

▲ *Peanut Buddy* - The Chestnut-backed Chickadees are the only chickadee species on Vancouver Island. They are the smallest member of their family and are named after their "chick-a-dee" call. Their diet includes insects, spiders and seeds. They are easily attracted to backyard feeders and can be trained to take peanuts from your hand.

▶ *Perpetual Motion* - Golden-crowned Kinglets are small, active birds that never stop moving. Both sexes have the golden crown but only the male has the red crest. They are constantly in motion as they glean insects and insect eggs from coniferous trees. They are year-round residents of the Pacific coast from California to Alaska.

▶ *Harry the Hummer* - Harry is the dominant male Rufous Hummingbird in my backyard. He usually arrives in the third week of March and waits for his harem of females. After a successful mating season, he has no patience for his offspring and usually disappears by late June.

Rufous Hummingbird in my backyard

Hermit Thrush at Fairwinds

Reclusive Thrush - Like the Varied and Swainson's Thrushes, the Hermit Thrush is very shy and prefers to stay away from people. It is usually found foraging in mixed coniferous and deciduous forests. In the spring it retreats to higher elevations.

▶ *What's Up Doc?* - Just another fly says the Pacific-slope Flycatcher as it contemplates another meal. Pacific-slope Flycatchers breed from B.C. south to California and winter on the Pacific Coast of Mexico.

▼ *Warbling Wonder* - The Warbling Vireo may be drab in appearance, but it is sparkling with its cheerful, warbling song. Foraging in dense foliage, it is often heard but not seen. It is fairly widespread as it breeds all across the U.S. and throughout western Canada. It winters in Mexico.

Pacific-slope Flycatcher
in my backyard

Warbling Vireo
at Dolphin Lake

Master Weaver - Bushtits are gregarious birds, travelling from bush to bush in large groups with other Bushtit families as they forage for worms and insects. They build delicate moss-covered, sock-like nests that hang from trees or bushes.

Bushtit in my backyard

Fitz - Bew - The familiar sound of the Willow Flycatcher is common on Vancouver Island for most of the spring and summer. Southern B.C. is the northern limit of the Willow's breeding range which covers most of the U.S. It winters along the coasts of Mexico, Central America, and northern South America.

▼ **Small Bird, Big Voice** - The deep, resonant voice and bold eye-ring are distinctive features of the petite Cassin's Vireo. It nests in southern B.C. and winters in Mexico.

Willow Fly-catcher at Legacy Marsh

Cassin's Vireo in my backyard

Laysan Albatross 80 km west of Tofino

Pelagic Magic

This section is dedicated to Ron and Hetty Mann. Thanks to their kindness and generosity, I was able to spend 13 days (May 26 - June 7/06) on board the Osprey I. While the Osprey I was fishing for hake 80 km west of Tofino, I was delirious with joy in pelagic bird heaven. It was a remarkable and unforgettable experience for which I will always be grateful.

■ *Pelagic Heaven* - Most people who look out to the Pacific see nothing but air, space, and as S. T. Coleridge put it, "Water, water everywhere nor any drop to drink." But there is more, much more. The Pacific is part of the global playground for an amazing array of pelagic birds from the gigantic albatrosses to the tiny storm petrels. Many pelagic birds spend most of their lives at sea and only come to land to breed.

■ *Big White* - The Laysan Albatross is one of the pelagic birds I was lucky to encounter 80 km west of Tofino. They are uncommon around Vancouver Island as they prefer to be further offshore and closer to Alaska. With wingspans of 195 cm (78 in), they are considered small albatrosses. Like most albatrosses their lives are spent at sea until it is time to breed. They reach sexual maturity in about 8 or 9 years. Their nesting grounds are in the Hawaiian archipelago.

Black-footed Albatross

■ Although there are only about 400,000 Black-footed Albatrosses in the world, the offshore waters of Vancou ver Island are part of their domain. There were about 300 around the Osprey I every day enjoying the steady stream of fish scraps being expelled from the hake processing plant. Their regular meals consist of fish, squid, and fish eggs. They reach sexual maturity in about 5 years and nest in Hawaii and Japan. Unfortunately, thousands are killed each year by drift nets and long line fishing.

■ *Shearwaters* - Like miniature albatrosses, they shear effortlessly through the air as they skim centimeters above the waves. They are the shearwaters, medium-sized pelagic birds with 120 centimeter wingspans. Like most pelagic birds, they have a single tube in their nostrils at the top of their bills which allows them to excrete excess salt from the salt water they drink. Born in the southern hemisphere, they migrate in the spring to their north Pacific feeding grounds.

The most abundant species are the Sooty and Short-tailed Shearwaters. The Osprey I was the vortex of action as hundreds swirled endlessly around the boat like a whirlwind. They would land on the water and sometimes dive under to retrieve submerged food, then take off and circle around for another feeding session.

Both are dark brown in colour, but the Sooty Shearwaters have sloped foreheads and longer bills. The Short-tailed Shearwaters have short, steep foreheads and smaller bills. Both species originate in the southern hemisphere with the Sooty having a more widespread breeding range off Australia, New Zealand, and South America. The Short-tailed Shearwaters only breed off southeastern Australia.

Two other species I saw west of Tofino were the Flesh-footed and Pink-footed Shearwaters. There was only one of the former and about 6 of the latter. The Flesh-footed is from Australia and New Zealand and is uncommon off Vancouver Island. The Pink-footed nests off Chile and small numbers are common close to Vancouver Island during the summer.

Flesh-footed Shearwaters are uncommon off V.I. as they prefer warmer waters and do not travel as far north as other shearwaters. Their diet of fish, squid, and crustaceans is similar to other shearwaters.

Short-tailed Shearwater

Sooty Shearwater

Pink-footed Shearwaters are the largest shearwater seen off Vancouver Island. They breed on the offshore islands of Chile where long underground burrows are excavated for nesting. The female lays one egg, and both parents share the incubation of the egg. With only about 90,000 birds in existence, Pink-footed Shearwaters are close to being an endangered species.

Offensive Defense - Beware of the Northern Fulmar as it has a secret weapon that must be avoided. When confronted by predators it ejects a foul vomit capable of destroying the waterproofing of a bird's feathers and causing drowning. The Northern Fulmar looks like a stocky, thick-necked gull but flies with a distinctive jerky, stiff-winged motion. Another feature is its downward pointing bill.

dark morph
Northern Fulmar

It is a bird of the Atlantic and Pacific coast and common offshore of Vancouver Island. Breeding takes place in colonies on cliffs in the Canadian high Arctic and the Bering Sea. The nest is simply a shallow scrape in the rocks where one egg is laid. It is incubated by both parents for about seven weeks, and the chick is nursed for another seven weeks before it is fledged.

Light morph
Northern Fulmar

Parasitic Jaeger

■ *Pirates of the Sea* - Could Black-beard have been reincarnated with wings? The answer would be "yes" if you have ever seen jaegers in action. Jaegers are quite capable of foraging for their own food, but they prefer to be pirates. The like to take food from others. Typically, they fly above a flock of foraging birds. When they spot a likely target, they dive-bomb, hoping to force the bird to drop its catch. This is called kleptoparasitism. The strategy is often successful, but sometimes it backfires if the target is an aggressive gull. This time it is the gull and its buddies that gang up on the jaeger to retrieve what's left of the catch.

Three species are seen offshore of Vancouver Island. From largest to smallest, they are the Pomarine (700 g - 1.5 lb), Parasitic (470 g - 1.0 lb), and Long-tailed (300 g - 11 oz) Jaegers. They are all guilty of varying degrees of kleptoparasitism, and they all nest on the Arctic tundra. While nesting, their main source of food is lemmings and voles. After breeding they migrate south to Mexico and South America where they spend most of their time at sea.

South Polar Skuas are bulky, broad-winged, and short-tailed gull-like birds that behave much like jaegers. At 1,450 g (3.2 lb), they are twice the weight of Pomarine Jaegers. Besides diving for fish or grabbing food from the surface, Skuas are also not above stealing from other birds. Unlike jaegers, they nest in Antarctica. The female usually lays two eggs and both parents share the incubation. They migrate north in a clockwise loop to Japan and then North America. The peak time for them to be in B.C. waters is August to October, but they are often seen as early as May.

Long-tailed Jaeger

Pomarine Jaeger

South Polar Skua

■ *A Pair of Pelagic Gulls* - The Sabine's Gull and Black-legged Kittiwake are small gulls that spend most of their lives at sea. Both nest in the Arctic, but the smaller Sabine's Gull nests on the tundra close to ponds or lakes in colonies often quite close to Arctic Tern colonies. The Black-legged Kittiwake nests on narrow ledges on rocky cliffs. Nesting for both species is usually finished by the end of July and the migration southward peaks in August and September. The Sabine's Gull goes as far south as Chile while the Black-legged Kittiwake goes as far as Mexico. Most of the migration is offshore and seldom seen from land.

Black-legged Kittiwake

Sabine's Gulls

Cassin's Auklet

◄ *Bump in the Night* - On my second night a sea, Steve, the first mate woke me at 2:00 A.M. to show me some warblers flying in the ship's lights. After the warblers left he was telling about birds that landed or crashed into the boat when he was interrupted by a "thump." We looked down to see a slightly stunned bird at our feet. We caught it to prevent further mishap and released it shortly afterwards. It was a new bird for both of us. Using my Sibley's field guide, Steve correctly identified it as a Cassin's Auklet.

Fork-tailed
Storm Petrel

◄ *Mosquito Birds* - Compared to the albatrosses, the Fork-tailed Storm Petrels seemed like little mosquitoes as they buzzed in and around the bigger birds to scavenge their share of fish scraps. But, they were far from little as their wingspans averaged 49 cm (19 in). They breed on small islets where they dig burrows or use cavities for their nests. They lay one egg and both parents share the incubation.

Lesser Nighthawk

◄ *A New Bird for B.C.* - On June 5 a small brown bird flew up to the Osprey I. I excitedly took as many pictures as possible as I knew it was something different and maybe special. From the pictures I could see that it was a nighthawk and simply assumed it was a Common Nighthawk. After I posted it on my website I started receiving emails correcting me. It was later confirmed to be a Lesser Nighthawk by experts on ID Frontiers as well as David Sibley. This was the first Lesser Nighthawk reported in B.C. The only other sighting in Canada was at Point Pelee National Park in 1974. Lesser Nighthawks are desert birds found in southern U.S. and the tropics.

Pacific Golden-Plover at Iona Park

Great Gray Owl
at U.B.C.

Western Bluebird at Vernon

Western Kingbird
at Vernon

McKay's Bunting
at Iona Park

126

Yellow-headed Blackbird at Kelowna

Mountain Bluebirds at Kelowna

Ruddy Duck at Kelowna

Bibliography

Baron, Nancy and Acorn, John. *Birds of Coastal British Columbia and the Pacific Northwest*. Vancouver: Lone Pine Publishing, 1997

Sibley, David Allen. *The Sibley Guide to Birds*. New York: Alfred A. Knopf, Inc., 2000

Internet Resources

Cornell Lab of Ornithology, 2003. *All About Birds, Online Bird Guide*. http://birds.cornell.edu

Bird Web. Seattle Audubon Society. http://birdweb.org

Dedication

To my mother, Mary, whose only concern in life has been the welfare of her family. She has always been supportive without questioning any of my choices in life. Perhaps she knew something that no one else knew when she gave me the middle name, "Robin."

Index